The Waterwheel

Practical Wisdom for 64 Common Concerns

Jill S. Woolworth, LMFT

Illustrated by Wajih Chaudhry

ISBN: 978-0-692-18430-1

Cardinal Flower Publishing
Greenwich, Connecticut
http://www.jillwoolworth.com

Book Designer: Vicky Vaughn Shea,
    Ponderosa Pine Design
Publishing Consultant: Holly Brady,
    Brady New Media Publishing

Address permission requests to:
info@jillwoolworth.com

To purchase multiple copies of this book at reduced prices:
info@jillwoolworth.com

Dedication

*To my three daughters, Jocelyn, Virginia and Helen,
and all of my "adopted daughters." You have poured
yourselves into my life in powerful ways.*

Contents

Preface . . . . *ix*

Introduction . . . . *xi*

Self-Talk

1. Life Is the Story We Tell Ourselves 1
2. No One Gets a Perfect 52-Card Deck 3
3. Love Your Body Before You Miss It 5
4. Full or Busy? 7
5. G.E.M.S. (Gratitude, Exercise, Meditation & Service) 9
6. Nature Right-Sizes Us 11
7. Mosaics & Seasons 13
8. Well-Being Is Equal Parts Comfort & Growth 15
9. A Playground, Not a Single Path 17
10. The House of Truth vs. The House of Lies 19
11. Take a Sabbatical 21
12. The Alphabet of Gratitude 23

Relationships

13. Swiss Cheese 27
14. Vulnerability Drops 29
15. Level Ground 31
16. Kindness 33
17. Relationships Trump Tasks 35
18. Christmas Trees 37
19. Banning B.A.N.S (But, Always, Never & Should) 39
20. A Picture Frame for Love 41

Difficult Situations

21. Boundaries Are Like Cells 45
22. Communication Is What's Received 47
23. Resent-o-Meter 49
24. Renting Brain Space 51
25. Bandaged in a Wheelchair 53
26. Learn the Story 55
27. The Elder Brother Cliff 57
28. Avoiding Triangles 59
29. Big, Ugly Earrings 61
30. Grace Sandwiches 63
31. Wagging Finger or Open Palm? 65
32. E.G.O.= Easily Gets Offended 67
33. A 10 Reaction to a 1 Infraction 69
34. The Pause 71
35. The Anger Cauldron 73

Losses

36. Love & Loss Are Twins 77
37. Grieving or Grievance? 79
38. A Grudge 81
39. Stars in a Dark Sky 83
40. Kintsukuroi 85
41. Sit in the Pit 87

Marriage/Partnering

42. Marriage Coaching 91
43. Below the Waterline 93
44. The Rejection Coin 95
45. The Marriage Castle 97
46. Ignorance, Not Malevolence 99
47. Connection & Safety 101
48. From Land Mines to the I.C.U. 103
49. Marriage 1.0. 2.0, 3.0 105
50. Cell Phones Can't Charge Each Other 107
51. L.O.V.E. (Listen, Open Space, Validate & Empathize) . . 109
52. Polka Dot Jackets 111
53. Costumes 113
54. The 1-to-10 Scale 115

Parenting

55. The Red Zone 119
56. Parent Your Best Friend's Child 121
57. Affirm, Affirm, Affirm 123
58. Health & Safety 125
59. Build a Team 127
60. If You Need an Answer Now, It's No 129
61. Rescues 131
62. A Tulip or an Oak Tree? 133
63. Luxuries & Emergencies 135
64. Changing the Legacy 137

Preface

I grew up in an old gristmill that had been converted into a house. As a child, I could see through tiny cracks in the living room walls to the outdoors where I spent most of my waking hours.

My brother and I lived outside in rain or shine. We explored the riverbanks, built forts, played house, and swam. At lunchtime, Mom often dropped a basket out of the dining room window to a platform next to the river. When leeches attached to our ankles, we took the Wesson Oil bottle from the kitchen shelf, inverted it to cover one leech at a time, and continued our conversation on the kitchen steps until they all detached. Mom used the same bottle for cooking.

Gristmills are powered by waterwheels that look like Ferris wheels. Instead of seats for people, their buckets harness the power of flowing water to turn the gears that grind grain into flour between large millstones. I sometimes imagine people as buckets on a multi-dimensional waterwheel, continuously moving through life's river of challenges, pouring themselves into each other and refreshing one another.

When I was young, I wanted to fill up my buckets—with love, material things, good grades, and food. Now that I am older, I want to share some of the experiences and wisdom that have been generously poured into me by many patient, wise people—including Gretchen, Bob, Elisabeth, John, Larry, Ian, Mel, Susan, Linda, Neely, Gordon, Jean, Gail, Heather, Don, Robbin, Crissy, Bill, Ellen, George, Lindsay and Lisa. The most important is my husband, Rick.

Other tributaries who have poured wisdom into me include my parents, my siblings, my grandparents, teachers, classmates and friends from childhood to adulthood, colleagues, clients, lecturers, and authors, many of whom are deceased and/or don't know me. I even include strangers whose comments or actions have touched me deeply. For all these human interactions, including those that were difficult, I am grateful.

— Jill S. Woolworth, Greenwich, Connecticut

Introduction

Human beings are not neatly divided into two camps, those who are mentally healthy and those who are mentally ill. Everyone sits somewhere on the spectrum of mental health. If I weren't a tad narcissistic, I wouldn't take time to put on makeup in front of a mirror each morning. I have generalized anxiety disorder, and yet I am a Licensed Marriage & Family Therapist (LMFT). We do the best we can with the understanding we have at the moment.

Over the last 25 years of leading small groups and working with clients, I have found that a non-pathological approach to mental health helps many people deal with life's challenges and transitions. Imagery, humor, and simple advice speak to us universally at all ages.

This book contains 64 whimsical illustrations of familiar life challenges followed by explanations and examples. The examples are compilations of true stories with important details changed. Many of the stories are my own. If you read "your story," it is because you are not alone.

In taking a lighthearted approach to many common experiences, I hope to normalize these experiences and offer practical wisdom for navigating life and relationships.

The illustrations introducing each idea are playful.

Playing is the way that we learn to do things differently. Children aren't afraid to try new things. Adults often are.

Throughout this book, you will discover new ways to be more understanding and effective when speaking to yourself and others. Each page offers an idea related to one of the following topics: self-talk, relationships, difficult situations, losses, marriage/partnering, and parenting.

I have witnessed people of all ages change in all kinds of challenging circumstances. I believe you can, too. Sometimes all you need is a shift in perspective. My hope is that, in the pages that follow, you will find ideas that open new doors for you.

Self-Talk

❶
Life Is the Story We Tell Ourselves

Choose your story wisely. Most of us have experienced significant challenges. How we tell our story to ourselves and to others matters. Do you plant the ladder of your story on the sinking sands of victimhood, or on the solid ground of survivorship? If you're reading this book, you are a survivor. Tell your story from that perspective. You will not diminish what happened; you will be telling the truth about the present.

How you tell your story changes the way your brain stores the information each time you tell it. You literally have the choice to lay new tracks over old in your memory. Stories of courage, hope, strength, and transformation reinforce your ability to continue taking courageous, hopeful, strong, transformative actions.

Kendall was terrified of the things her ex-husband said about her and of the awful things he might do. For years, she told her story from the perspective of a helpless victim. With coaching, she learned to share her story as a courageous survivor. She was amazed by her new abilities to pay less attention to his threats, to land a more lucrative job, to raise their children, and to develop a large network of supportive and fun-loving friends.

2

No One Gets a Perfect 52-Card Deck

No one gets a perfect 52-card deck in life. We all have setbacks, disappointments and parts of our lives we wish were different. Whether these challenges are minor or serious, the same question applies: how will you play the cards you were dealt? An overweight person might trade the A's she earned in school to be thin. An attractive man might trade his good looks for more intelligence or athletic ability. Someone with difficult parents or siblings might trade them for "the perfect family."

Your cards are your cards. Some of them are gifts. Some aren't. What will you do with them? Blaming someone else won't change the cards you hold. Some of your difficult cards may turn out to be the most valuable ones in your life. It's your move.

Heather was physically abused as a child. She now writes music and poetry. She speaks in public forums and blogs about the issues that caused her so much pain. In so doing, she is turning her worst card into a gift for others, while she heals herself.

Parker hated his learning difference. He was often teased in childhood. Now as a beloved teacher at a school for children with learning differences, he knows that his personal experience is one of the reasons his students trust him.

3

Love Your Body Before You Miss It

Speak appreciatively to your reflection in the mirror. In 10 years, you'll miss the body you have now. No body ever changes in response to disparagement. Talk about your body as you would want a friend to talk about his or hers. Consider people listening, especially your friends and your children. If you are unkind in the ways you speak about your body, chances are your friends and your children will speak unkindly about their own.

Put exercise and other forms of self-care that you enjoy on your calendar as you would any other appointment. You are worth it. Your body has literally been supporting you all your life. It works hard.

Marta is more comfortable with her body at 55 than she was when she was younger. She finally likes her body and wishes that she had appreciated her younger body more. She regrets that she let a number on a scale determine her self-worth. She doesn't call herself "bad" anymore when she eats something delicious and caloric.

Gil often spoke disparagingly about his extra pounds before his heart attack at 44. Now he talks about how grateful he is to be alive. He congratulates himself for working out three times a week and chooses his meals more thoughtfully. He has never felt better.

4

Full or Busy?

We feed each other anxiety pills when we talk about our "busy" lives. Busy makes our egos puff up and blow harder to fight our common fear of inadequacy.

Talking about a "full" life is more positive. A full life is peaceful; it nourishes a sense of abundance, and it offers the option to add or subtract activities from your schedule. When you talk about your full life, your activity level doesn't change—only your experience of it. A busy life can control you. But a full life, you control.

The words we choose influence how we feel about ourselves and others. People who make a habit of substituting "full" for "busy" feel less anxious and more productive.

Raj was a frantic executive who described himself as "crazy busy." When he began to substitute the word "full" for "busy," he noticed that he was calmer. The only change Raj made was his use of this one word. He shares his reasoning with anyone who asks. Most have never thought about the difference. Those who copy him and make the switch from "busy" to "full" are grateful.

5

G.E.M.S.

G.E.M.S.—Gratitude, Exercise, Meditation and Service—are simple things we can do for ourselves when we're feeling disconnected or discouraged. G.E.M.S. raise our bodies' natural levels of dopamine, serotonin, oxytocin and endorphins—our bodies' feel-good chemicals. Best of all, G.E.M.S. are immediately available and free of cost.

It is impossible to be anxious and grateful at the same time. The neurons in your brain fire in either one direction or the other. If you name three things you are grateful for when you sense anxiety creeping in, you will gently shift the blood flow in your brain. Do this before you go to bed and you will sleep better.

You don't have to run a race to get a runner's high. Exercise in any form works. Dancing, walking, yoga, even climbing a flight of stairs benefits your mind and body. Meditation activates the calming part of your nervous system. It helps you *respond* to life, rather than *react* to it. Service—doing something for someone else—activates the parts of our brain that feel connected to others, and purposeful.

G.E.M.S. can travel with you wherever you go. Jenna, a college student, referred to gratitude, exercise, meditation and service as "the gems in my pocket" during her study abroad, valuable tools she could use to handle the normal fears and anxieties that come from being in a new place.

6

Nature Right-Sizes Us

Indoor spaces can make us forget our true size. We can swell to larger-than-life with a recent accomplishment or shrink to insignificance with a disappointment. When we are indoors, our appearance and our performance are often evaluated, either by ourselves or by others. It is easy to feel too big or too small.

Walking in the woods, in the mountains, on a beach, or even around the block restores us to our true size. Nature does not evaluate us. There is no need to look a certain way or to do more than put one foot in front of the other. Being in nature causes blood to flow away from the parts of our brain that brood over things we cannot change. Solitude, silence, and slowing our pace can restore a sense of well-being.

Brad shuts down his laptop when it needs to reboot. For the same reason, he takes 10 minutes to walk outside every day at lunchtime. Even in the cityscape where he works, fresh air and the occasional tree remind him that there is life beyond his deadlines, his financial concerns, and the challenges of raising children. Nature reboots his brain.

(7)

Mosaics & Seasons

Most people's lives and careers are more like mosaics than straight lines. All those "wasted or wandering" periods we worry about are actually part of life's beauty. Over the years, the stories we share from our most challenging seasons allow us to connect deeply with each other. There is no single path in our lives that we must "find."

However, healthy meandering is not passive. It requires actively paying attention to and accepting where we are in the moment in order to move forward with confidence.

Rather than trying to engineer our perfect pathway and outcome, we can learn to expect twists and turns, surprises, and closed doors, as well as new opportunities as they arise.

Alex thought everything had to be done in one season, especially during her 20's and 30's. Learning to trust that the pieces would cohere when she looked back on her life was hard for her. Now that she is 60, she is surprised by the variety of things she has done. At age 21, her circuitous path would have made no sense. It does in hindsight.

Yours will, too.

8

Well-Being Is Equal Parts Comfort & Growth

Too much "comfort" leads to boredom. Too much "growth" causes chronic anxiety. Comfort is sameness, routine, and predictability. Growth includes change, learning, losses, and challenge. We need both.

Our lives are rarely a perfect 50/50 blend. Moving to a new community, starting a new job, starting or ending a relationship can feel like 95 percent growth and 5 percent comfort. Big changes are difficult. Our brains are wired to fear change and stay with the familiar to keep us safe.

During seasons of change, give yourself as much comfort as possible.

Ella got a new job in a new city. She missed her friends. She was relieved to learn that feeling uncomfortable during a season of growth was normal. She discovered that sadness and anxiety were rich states of mind, not something she needed to escape from or medicate. For comfort, she pampered herself and savored connections with old friends by phone.

⑨

A Playground, Not a Single Path

There is no single path that will lead us to a well-crafted life.

Children have latitude to swing on the swings, play in the sandbox, or jump on the trampoline. So do adults. Why not try out the jungle gym, or climb the slide backwards? The boundaries of our playgrounds are clear—they are the fences made of our values. We can explore without fear.

A variation of this "playground" concept is "trying on dresses in a store." How will we know if we like a new job or a new behavior until we try it on? In a store we feel no anxiety when we reject an item of clothing after trying it on. We learn from whatever we "try on"—even if we end up discarding it.

Amon gave himself permission to "play" by taking different night courses before deciding on a major career change.

Kate gave herself permission to approach each date as a "play date," instead of as a pre-marital assessment task.

🔟

The House of Truth vs. The House of Lies

Most of us wander back and forth across the psychological road between the House of Truth and the House of Lies. This can happen many times during the same day. Negative messages draw us into the House of Lies without our even noticing it. There, anxiety is the wallpaper and depression is the flooring. The scent of fear permeates the house. Our reflections in the distorted mirrors tell us we're unlovable, unworthy, too much, or too little.

Wise friends and mentors help us spend more time in the House of Truth where the solid floor of honesty, the artwork of the beauty of creation, and the comfortable chair of acceptance invite us to feel at home. While there may be thoughts and behaviors that you want to change in the House of Truth, situations are manageable, and change is possible.

"I overeat 24/7," moaned Angela. Her therapist responded, "Well, at least for this hour you'll have a break. Did you overeat this morning? Are you a middle-of-the-night eater? How hard is lunchtime?" Initially put off by her therapist's questions, Angela moved from the House of Lies to the House of Truth when she realized that she overeats only between 5 and 7 pm. Then she and her therapist were able to develop strategies for coping with one-twelfth of her day.

⑪
Take a Sabbatical

Do you ever wonder if you are addicted to a certain behavior? Can you live without your cell phone for an afternoon, alcohol each night, your shopping habit, video games? If not, experiment with taking periodic "sabbaticals." (One woman refers to hers as "spa vacations.") These timeouts—when framed in positive language—make a change in behavior feel like a privilege, rather than a deprivation or punishment.

Also, share your intent with one trustworthy friend. Talking honestly about the behavior that bothers you reduces its power considerably. The old adage is true: *we are only as sick as our secrets.*

If periodic sabbaticals aren't sustainable, you'll have a clue that you need more support to "let go" of the behavior. Remember, you're choosing to "let it go," rather than to have it "taken away," or "giving it up." Sabbaticals from behaviors give us important information about ourselves while opening up productive space to focus on other interests.

James takes periodic sabbaticals from alcohol, Susannah from spending money, and Justin from screen time. Knowing that they can successfully and happily put boundaries around their behaviors is a gift they give themselves.

⑫
The Alphabet of Gratitude

It's worth repeating that we can't be anxious and grateful at the same time. Expressing gratitude for anything reboots our brains out of fight-or-flight mode. Writing five things we are grateful for in a journal or saying them out loud is comfort food for our brains.

Sometimes a journal isn't handy and speaking aloud isn't an option. We might be on a crowded subway or sleeping with our partner in the room. Especially in the middle of the night when blood sugar is lowest and anxiety is likely highest, we can lower our anxiety by mentally running through an alphabet of friends we have loved, places we've enjoyed, or foods we appreciate. (We can skip letters we can't find a name for. Few of us have been to Zanzibar, adore zucchini, or have a friend named Xerxes.) This practice usually puts us back to sleep before the third iteration.

Along with using the alphabet of gratitude, Jennifer and Ryan practice sharing "three gratitudes" at bedtime. These are the last things they say to each other before they roll over to sleep. Each gratitude is something special that happened during the day—a conversation, a sunset, a good report. Their brief expressions of gratitude calm their brains and help them fall asleep more easily.

Relationships

⑬

Swiss Cheese

We prefer to look like solid blocks of cheddar cheese perfection, but it is through the Swiss cheese holes of our humanity that we connect with each other. It is healthy to let others who have earned our trust see our vulnerabilities.

Cheddar cheeses are lonely. Swiss cheeses are relatable. Our closest friends are those we have invited to see through our "holes." They see us! This is true intimacy. Trustworthy people celebrate our accomplishments and, more importantly, comfort, encourage, and challenge us during times of loss and discouragement. We do the same for them.

André avoided risk and strangers. He liked being a wall of cheddar. His solid wall felt like protection—armor developed during a difficult childhood. In professional settings, his armor worked well, but André was lonely. He wanted a life partner and closer friendships. As he developed the courage to reveal his true self through his human "holes," he grew closer to his friends and found a partner.

🔢 Vulnerability Drops

Titration is the chemical process of slowly adding drops of one substance into a test tube containing another substance until a certain reaction occurs. Sharing our personal stories deserves a similar careful process. People haven't earned the right to know our whole story when they first meet us. What works best is when we share a few drops of vulnerability at a time—and wait to see if our gesture is well received and reciprocated.

Another way to imagine this process is as a fisherman baiting a hook, hoping a fish will bite.

Think of intimacy as "into-me-see." In order to develop healthy intimacy, it helps to choose our friends thoughtfully and test them as we go. We can become more sensitive to our own level of willingness to share, and let others see into us gradually. Sharing our vulnerability is the key to whole-hearted living. For best results, it happens slowly.

David and Eric decided to share a dream, a goal, a disappointment, and a fear with each other. Each of these things was a vulnerability drop. As a result, their friendship deepened.

⑮

Level Ground

A skilled professional understands that her clients' life experiences are just as important as her own professional expertise. She meets her clients on level ground. Wise leaders do the same with their subordinates.

It is hard to trust a person who towers over others, or one who looks down at us from a lofty platform of expertise or judgment. Level ground is the best place for trustworthy relationships, including professional ones. Level ground is about attitude, not knowledge.

We communicate our attitude by word choices, tone of voice, and especially body position. Others stay calmer when we are eye to eye with them because we are no longer intimidating. Overriding our desire to impress is a powerful way of showing compassion.

Sarah had to fire her employee. Beth was an oncologist with bad news. Both left their desks and took chairs facing the people to whom they were bringing bad news. Being face to face made their difficult messages easier to hear.

Zach sat on a stair below his disobedient four-year-old so that he could look into his son's eyes. When he did so, his anger softened and his son was better able to listen because Daddy was no longer twice as tall as he was.

🄰 Kindness

Kindness is the most important character trait of all. It cannot be put on like a shirt for a special occasion because it develops through repeated daily decisions to think and act kindly. Kindness is a key quality to look for in all relationships, especially in a mate.

Pay attention to how you and others treat the less powerful or socially awkward—the needy friend, the elderly grandparent, waitstaff, rambunctious children, grumpy customers, and bad drivers—just to name a few. These often-overlooked situations can reveal and help us measure kindness both in others and in ourselves.

When Sasha was in college, her boyfriend came to the house where she was babysitting to help her care for two little kids. As she bathed the older girl in the bathroom, she overheard his kind, playful voice as he fed dinner to the one-year-old in his high chair. She remembers thinking that she wanted this man to be the father of her children. He is.

⑰
Relationships Trump Tasks

Most people would agree that their relationships are more important than daily tasks, but our academic training and the demands of work teach us to prioritize tasks over relationships. Making space in our schedules for relationships is a lifelong discipline that pays rich dividends. Human relationships are living "things" that require attention, time, light, and nourishment. They are worth more than income or fame.

When we make a phone call, play with our child, date our spouse, celebrate or console a friend—especially when that friend is ill or has a loss, that person is unlikely to forget what we did. People's end-of-life regrets are more often about relationships not attended to than accomplishments not achieved.

Consider what five things you want said about yourself on your 80th birthday. These are your goalposts, the buoys by which to navigate your life. For 99 percent of people, good relationships top accomplishments on the list.

After bragging about his professional accomplishments, a 40-year-old executive in marital crisis realized that he wanted his wife at his 80th birthday party more than he wanted his long line of potential girlfriends. He began prioritizing his marital relationship, and he is still married.

18

Christmas Trees

A Christmas tree is glittery and beautiful, and unaware that it has been cut off just above the roots. Similarly, we humans enjoy decorating ourselves with clothing, social status, accomplishments, and possessions. It is good to enjoy these things. Just remember that they are decorations. They are not our real substance.

Friendship, family, faith, and service to others—these are substance, not decoration. They are the roots that help us flourish. They provide meaning, connection, and purpose.

Fashions and fame, like decorated Christmas trees, are only with us for a season. People of substance, like healthy trees, grow for many years and give shelter and shade to others.

Alyssa refers to friends who remind her of Christmas trees as "shiny people." These are people she can't get close to because they are intent on impressing her with their beautiful lives. She decided for herself to focus on being a blessing to her friends instead of impressing them. As she did so, the roots of her confidence and well-being grew deeper.

⑲

Banning B.A.N.S.

The words *but, always, never,* and *should* (which form the acronym B.A.N.S.) too often close off options for ourselves and for others. In contrast, *rarely, sometimes, often,* and *frequently* are usually closer to the truth and leave the door open for change. Banning B.A.N.S is a way to be kinder and more honest with ourselves and others.

For example, the word *but* negates anything we say right before it. "I love you, *but* we don't do fun things together" triggers the listener's fear and defensiveness. Substituting *and* for *but*—"I love you, *and* I want to do fun things together"—is much more likely to lead to fun.

When we say *I want to* or *I'd like to* instead of *I should, I must,* or *I ought to,* there's a better chance we'll actually do something. "*I want to* exercise more" works in the part of our brain that senses pleasure and fun. The self-critical statement "*I should* exercise more" triggers fear.

Carlos never got it right, and Joy always nagged. After a period of counseling, they were surprised to hear each other say that sometimes he got it right, and sometimes she didn't nag. They made a practice of noticing and telling each other when he got it right and she wasn't nagging. They gained confidence. Over time Carlos got it right more and more often, and Joy rarely nagged.

20

A Picture Frame for Love

Sometimes our concern about how we look or how we are perceived gets in the way of connecting with people. When we draw attention to our "frame" and worry about how we are perceived, we forget about the gift of love that our simple presence can offer.

Pay attention to the people around you. Take the imaginary camera off yourself at your next social gathering. Ask questions. Find the lonely person. Taking a genuine interest in other people quiets our nervous self-consciousness, enhances our sense of well-being, and benefits others.

Two gifted speakers talked about faith to large groups. Avery was personal, funny and brilliant. She invited the audience into her open picture frame of God's love. The audience was encouraged and inspired. Jess was equally eloquent and knowledgeable, but her comments about her dress, her jewelry, and her vacations prevented her listeners from getting beyond her frame to her message.

In his late 80's, Ivan raised money and awareness for a post-incarceration support program. He became the quiet frame for the people he helped. They were the focal point of his picture.

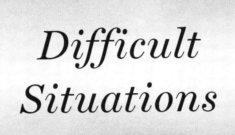

Difficult
Situations

㉑
Boundaries Are Like Cells

A healthy cell in our bodies allows in what is nourishing and keeps out what is unhealthy. An unhealthy cell doesn't have that ability, which can lead to cancer. Boundaries work similarly in human relationships. All of us have had our boundaries violated, some more seriously than others. We can guard against being permeable to toxic relationships by paying close attention to what we allow into and exclude from our lives. Our health depends on it.

Unhealthy friends may call frequently for advice or to complain repeatedly about the same thing. They may tell us that we are the only one who understands. Our egos can be easily seduced. After months or years of listening and being frustrated that nothing changes, we accumulate toxicity. Limiting our contact to common courtesy—occasional phone calls, cards, and texts—is hard, but life-giving. Our friend will find other sources of support. He or she may or may not become healthier, but you definitely will.

Gray did everything he could for his friend Nick, but Nick's requests for money and his ranting about problems didn't end. Gray felt discouraged and stressed after their conversations. After several years, Gray ended their friendship when he moved to a new city. He still talks to Nick on occasion, but he is wary of engaging beyond a casual check-in.

❷❷

Communication Is What's Received

Communication is what's received, not what we intend. If we don't take responsibility for how we deliver our message, it might as well be lost in the mail. When communication goes awry, we often blame the recipient for not listening. But this is as useless as blaming someone for not receiving a letter. If our tone of voice, body language, or choice of words is off-putting, it is up to us to try again in a different way.

If a person thinks that a message of criticism is coming, that there's "a bomb in the mailbox," she will run. When a person anticipates being told that he has messed up or neglected something, his normal human response is to escape or defend himself. In moments of perceived threat, our brains default to fear, rarely assuming the other person's good intentions.

Sydney and Adam learned how to tell each other specifically what they wanted. They grew closer as they practiced new ways to communicate. "It would mean the world to me . . ." became an introduction that made them both laugh and made it highly likely the other would comply. "When you compliment me in front of your friends, I feel like your hero." "You doing the laundry is the sexiest thing in the world." They agree that tone matters, and that there is no such thing as an over-appreciated spouse (or colleague or employee).

㉓

Resent-o-Meter

Resentment is a blinking yellow light that indicates a change is needed. When we feel resentful, either someone is pushing against our boundaries, or we feel entitled to something unrealistic, such as a perfect (fill in the blank).

Pay attention to resentment: don't wish it away. It will not disappear or evaporate. We store it in our bodies. Long-term resentment, expressed outwardly, ultimately leads to verbal or physical explosions; expressed inwardly, it leads to various forms of self-harm, including depression. Do you need to clarify a boundary? Or change an entitled attitude?

Brandon and Chris had young children. Every year they invited Brandon's mother to visit for three weeks. Grandma tended to overrule Chris and dote on her son, and she was critical of the couple's parenting and lifestyle. This led to Brandon and Chris fighting most nights in their bedroom. With coaching, the couple was able to set clearer boundaries with Grandma: she was to affirm both parents, support their parenting, offer no unsolicited advice, and make visits shorter. Their family and their marriage benefited. Grandma adjusted.

㉔
Renting Brain Space

We own all the storage capacity in our brains. What stories do we want to store there by telling them again and again? Are we the hero, the survivor, the observer, or the victim of these stories? Do we really want to give difficult people a central room in our brain? This is our choice.

We have the power to re-wire our brains: we can either feed or starve our thoughts as they arise. Thoughts that we feed reconsolidate our memories and our emotional experiences every time we dwell on them. Thoughts that we starve lose their power.

There is no point in being hard on ourselves when negative thoughts arise. They will come. Imagine them like a cold fog: annoying, but not life-changing. The fog will pass. Even after years of thinking and feeling a certain way, we can choose to let thoughts go and set ourselves free.

Maria was angry at the way a school official had mistreated her daughter. Her point was valid, but after two years, she evicted the official from space in her brain when she realized that her anger was only affecting her. He was oblivious to her concern and might as well be "dancing through a field of daisies." Her daughter had moved on. Once Maria did too, she no longer suffered an unwelcome tenant in her brain.

25

Bandaged in a Wheelchair

Visualizing difficult people in our lives as "injured" can often help us cope, because they truly are "injured" insofar as they relate to us. Of course, they don't know this, and we have learned that telling them so doesn't help either of us.

Visualizing difficult people in humorous ways can also work. Imagining a boss as a petulant four-year-old with pigtails, a demanding parent as a mummy in a wheelchair, or an annoying relative as a hippo bellowing in the mud can help us smile instead of scream. Both approaches take away the power of the difficult person and calm our fearful brains.

We can also limit our exposure to these people, showing only common courtesy unless the toxic relationship changes. We can pray for them from an emotional distance, and for ourselves as we seek wisdom to understand our own part in the dynamic of the relationship, the only part we can change.

Christina pictured her controlling mother in a straitjacket. Jonathan pictured his angry father on a hospital bed with his leg in traction. Laura and Gabe pictured Gabe's intrusive mother as a monkey banging two cymbals. These images kept them all from taking other people's difficult behavior personally.

26

Learn the Story

Age 10 | Age 40

Hurt people hurt people. No one chooses to be hurt; however, all of us have some degree of injury from experiences of loss and rejection. It helps to take the time to understand our own stories. If our stories focus on blaming others or circumstances, we can rewrite them with professional help. Children who are abused often need coaching to not repeat the pattern they learned. Whatever we don't transform, we will transmit.

All behavior makes sense when we understand a person's story, including our own. The behavior may not be legal or moral, or even something we can tolerate, but learning others' stories will take away our judgment card and help us make wiser decisions about how to interact with people who do or say hurtful things. It will also free our brain space for more productive purposes.

Loading her suitcase in the overhead bin of an airplane, Meghan lightly grazed the head of a woman seated on the aisle. The woman screamed as if Meghan had hit her. People glared. After a short apology, Meghan sat for 25 minutes before tapping the woman ever so gently on the arm to ask her how her head was feeling. The woman replied, "I'm sorry I yelled like that. My head has been so tender since I started chemotherapy." Meghan learned the story of the woman's cancer treatment. She was free to feel compassion.

The Elder Brother Cliff

In the biblical story of the prodigal son, the elder brother is the one who does everything right and his younger brother does everything wrong. When the younger brother comes home from squandering his inheritance, his forgiving father throws him a banquet. The elder brother thinks this is unfair and refuses to come to the party.

When we think we are in the right, we often feel good for a while up on the cliff, but it's lonely. Stewing on the cliff of self-righteous superiority does not make relationships better. Come down to level ground and listen to the other person's story.

A person's behavior may be illegal, immoral, or reprehensible. We may ultimately choose not to be in relationship with that person. However, by getting off the elder-brother cliff, we may also move beyond anger and judgment to feel sadness and compassion.

After a year of meeting together, members of a small group were bothered by one another's "quirks." Then each member was given 45 uninterrupted minutes to share his life story. This experience was most memorable because these stories effectively replaced annoyance with empathy.

28

Avoiding Triangles

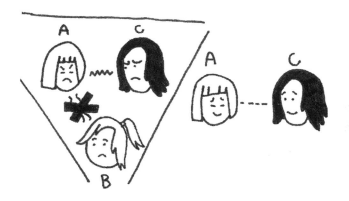

Amanda and Casey argue. Amanda calls Beth to complain about Casey. Beth's best bet is to duck the triangle and avoid being sucked into a "helper role." When she suggests that Amanda work it out directly with Casey, everyone benefits. Exceptions would be if Amanda is truly powerless to help herself, or if Beth has a professional responsibility to manage the relationship between Amanda and Casey.

Triangles are unhealthy in most relationships, but they are especially dangerous in nuclear families with siblings and adult children.

When you need advice or a place to vent, it's helpful to limit sharing to the smallest possible number of trustworthy friends. This limited sharing can help calm your mind and reboot your perspective. Then your work is best done directly with the offending party.

After years of feeling obligated to help, Anthony, the eldest in a family of six, realized that he was not helping and refused to participate when his siblings called to complain about each other. His siblings continued to try to bring him in, but he was firm. When he avoided family triangles, his life became more peaceful.

Nadia believed she had to be the go-between for disputes between her adult daughter and her ex-husband. When she gave up this role, her daughter grew stronger.

Big, Ugly Earrings

Imagine someone says to you, "Those are the biggest, ugliest earrings I have ever seen!" Confronting that person's rudeness directly or disagreeing with her could easily escalate into an argument. "Oh, I *do* have on big earrings today" is a response that avoids a confrontation.

Whenever we can agree with *even a small part* of what someone else is saying, it calms our nervous system and defuses the energy behind the other person's comment. It is literally disarming. The other person will feel heard—and perhaps surprised.

We all stumble into saying the wrong thing sometimes. Let's give ourselves and others a second chance. (Of course, if the hurtful language is abusive, repetitive, or contemptuous, we need a different strategy.)

Cameron's teenaged son, Liam, complained, "You are always late to pick me up." Cameron wisely avoided reacting to the word "always." He was late that day. Instead, he countered with, "You're right. I am late sometimes." Liam felt heard and was open to hearing the reasons why Cameron sometimes arrives late.

30

Grace Sandwiches

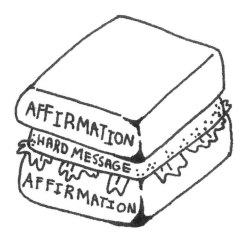

All of us have to communicate difficult messages. Rather than avoiding the issue until we escape or explode, we can build a "grace sandwich" with affirmation as bread.

The first slice of bread affirms the other person. Start by noting anything that he or she has done that you appreciate. This could be either a character quality or a specific action. Such statements calm our nervous systems and draw the listener's attention. We are all hungry for compliments.

Then add: "What I want to say isn't easy. I'm concerned you may be upset. And I need your help to get this right." Asking for help defuses defensiveness. Once you've done that, state the meat of the issue: the hard message.

The second slice of bread affirms the importance of your relationship, along with your confidence that the other person will do the right thing. Even if we doubt that he or she will, the odds of it happening increase between two slices of affirmation.

Blake declared to Olivia: "I was proud to tell my parents about the award you got at work. You deserved it. I'm lucky to have such a smart wife. I have an important request and I need your help. // I doubt you know how much it bothers me when I find your dishes in the sink. I feel like your maid. Please put them in the dishwasher. // Our relationship is the most important thing in the world to both of us. I know you want me to be happy. Thanks for listening.

㉛
Wagging Finger or Open Palm?

Any demand can be stated as a request. The problem is, most of us wait too long to make our wishes known, hoping that the other person will intuit our requests. Partners aren't mind readers. Neither are roommates.

It's important to communicate our requests before resentment builds up. It's easier to choose the right words and tone of voice when we're not angry. Otherwise, out comes our wagging finger, our sharp tongue, or maybe even a verbal hammer.

It's also important to find out the other person's preferred form of communication. One person might prefer a written list; another person might perceive such a list as nagging.

When our partner experiences us as an angry, critical authority figure instead of a peer with a sincere request for help, we usually get nowhere. Our partner's perception is reality regardless of our intent. Open palms have a higher hit-ratio than wagging fingers.

Sophia learned how to distinguish whether her partner, Scott, saw a wagging finger or an open palm by carefully observing his body movements as she made her requests. Scott moved toward her open palm and away from her wagging finger. She started over when she sensed Scott moving away.

E.G.O. = Easily Gets Offended

Our E.G.O., which Easily Gets Offended, can get us into a lot of relationship trouble. Our pride builds armor around us that we hope is impenetrable, but it isn't. People are inevitably going to do things that offend us. We offend others, too.

Taking offense is related to the Greek word *skandalon*, the trigger of a trap on which bait is placed for an animal. Though more closely related to our modern word *scandal*, *skandalon* is also translated as "a stumbling block or a snare."

When we take offense, we get our leg caught in a trap. An analogous image is biting down on a fish hook. The trapper and the fisherman may not even know that we've been caught! Research shows that we are most often unaware when we offend others. The degree to which we are not easily offended may be a barometer of our psychological and spiritual health.

Lydia was often the target of her mother's rampages. She couldn't escape. When these moments occurred, she imagined she was holding a bullfighter's red cape out to her side for her mother's rage to tear through. In this way, her ego didn't get gored, though sometimes Lydia did get nicked.

㉝

A 10 Reaction to a 1 Infraction

Having a "10" reaction to a "1" infraction is usually a reaction to old pain, probably from childhood. If we feel betrayed, abandoned, rejected, insulted, or misunderstood, and our reaction sucks more energy out of us than we want to expend, it helps to ask ourselves when we first experienced similar feelings. Chances are, we were powerless children then. We are adults now.

When the intensity of our response is out of proportion to the "1" infraction, it helps to ask ourselves: how do we—as grown-ups—want to respond? As adults, we have the ability to override our responses rooted in childhood trauma and lay down new memory track. With intentionality and practice, we can teach ourselves to have "1" reactions, even when they weren't modeled for us.

When Tiffany was 19, the man in the seat next to her on a small plane offered to put her backpack in the overhead bin. As he did so, the blueberry yogurt in the side pocket of Tiffany's backpack exploded on his white shirt. His calm "1" reaction to this event amazed her even more when she learned that he was a college president en route to give a speech. Years later, as CEO of a company, she shared this lesson with her team.

34

The Pause

When confronted with something difficult or unpleasant, pause before responding. A pause allows blood to flow back to our prefrontal cortex where logic, reason, compassion, and creativity help us formulate better responses. Without a pause, we're stuck in our reptilian brain with its fight-or-flight response, which is neither pretty nor productive.

Our pause button gets bigger with practice. Try breathing three times deeply to tell your nervous system that this is not a life-or-death emergency. We can sometimes buy ourselves a little more time by heading to a bathroom or bedroom.

Eve had an eating disorder. She thought that cookies ran straight off the grocery shelf into her mouth. Having grown up in a chaotic home, Eve had no idea she could cultivate a pause button. Over time, she learned to pause before making food choices. Her newfound ability to pause also helped her better handle relationships and important decisions.

The Anger Cauldron

Anger is not bad. It can be a helpful barometer to show us when change is needed. Problems arise when we store anger without understanding it. Most of us have trouble looking into our own anger cauldron, but if we don't, our anger can heat up.

When we or someone we love flies off the handle, it helps to look under the lid of anger for the hurt, the pain, the fear, or the sadness that has not been addressed—that has boiled over. There is always some form of "sad" under "mad." If our lids fly off repeatedly, smacking those we love in the face, professional support can help us figure out what kind of old pain is hiding in our cauldron.

Anger frightens all of us. We typically move *toward* another person's pain or sadness because we want to help, but fury usually *pushes us away*, just when we or someone we love needs help the most.

Trevor and Karen were out of control with anger. Their counselor asked them to hold hands and look silently into each other's eyes for 60 seconds without breaking eye contact. Those 60 seconds became sacred space. They both cried. They saw the hurt, the pain, and the sadness in each other's cauldron. Their voices quieted, and they embraced.

Losses

Love and Loss Are Twins

Loss in life is inevitable. Living things change, often not on our timetable. People we love die or move away. Others disappoint us or cause us suffering. Sometimes we disappoint ourselves. This is normal, not something to be medicated or hidden away.

Appropriately sharing our losses is gold for our psyches, as hard as this may be in the moment. The people we will cherish most are those who accept their losses, their fallibility, and their suffering, and use these experiences to become humble helpers of others.

Even happy events often include loss. When Ryan's daughter married and moved two thousand miles away, he was surprised that he grieved. As much as he celebrated his daughter's marriage and admired his son-in-law, he was losing something precious to him. The same is true for every parent who leaves a child at summer camp or college. Our babies grow up and leave us when we do our job well.

37

Grieving or Grievance?

Grieving is fluid and moves into acceptance and action on our unique timetable. No one can rush it. Grieving is normal for a year or more after a major loss. Feeling sad, bargaining with fate, waves of anger, and periods of depression are common experiences. Accepting the new normal takes time. Sometimes we hide from our friends or act out in uncharacteristic ways when we're grieving. There is no right way to grieve.

A grievance, on the other hand, grows inside us like a tumor, toxic to body and spirit. When our grieving becomes a grievance, our grievance defines our life. Grievances harden around us and suffocate our potential for experiencing hope and joy.

Mackenzie is an unhappily married woman who comments routinely about how difficult her life is because of what she perceives her impossible husband does or doesn't do. Her friends have given up trying to help her. When asked how her life would be different if he weren't so difficult, she can't even consider the question. She resumes her litany of complaints. Her huge list of grievances strangles her creative thinking.

38

A Grudge

Grudges, like grievances, are ugly, disgusting creatures. Who would want to hold one, let alone nurse one? No one is changed by our grudges except us. They eat at us so slowly we sometimes don't realize that they are consuming us whole.

Grudges feed on un-forgiveness. They lock us into a prison cell along with the offending party, who is only truly there in our imagination. We can open the cell door from the inside, but only when we are willing to let the "guilty party" out first. This doesn't mean minimizing the offense or excusing it—only letting go of feeding it. The key is in our hands; it's our decision, in our own time.

Wanting to get out of that jail and to let our grudge go can take a long time—sometimes years. The alternative is that the "guilty party" continues to expand and fill the cell of our mind. When we let our grudge go, we find that we have more productive ways to use that brain space.

Charlie's hatred of his verbally abusive father was "eating him up." His therapist asked him if he could recall a single happy scene with him. He remembered the time his dad brought him a puppy. The counselor asked him to fully describe the scene and bring it to mind every time he thought of his dad. At first Charlie was resistant, but over time, this practice changed the way he perceived him. His grudge disappeared.

39

Stars in a Dark Sky

When losses happen, it is natural to feel that nothing will ever be the same. It won't. The world seems a dark, endless black space. At some point, after the initial shock, it helps to schedule a few things on our calendar that will not replace the loss, but that could offer us comfort, companionship, or distraction, nevertheless. A date with a friend, a trip, or a cultural experience are all good choices. These are stars in our dark skies.

Depression after loss is normal and hits everyone between the "i's" of isolation and immobility. Putting stars in our skies pushes gently back on both. Even one star is a step toward our new life.

Ashley was a widow in a wheelchair. She saw no stars in her sky. With encouragement, she planned a birthday trip with a friend to a concert that she had dreamed of attending in a city an hour away. She hired a driver and a special car to accommodate her wheelchair. Planning for the occasion brought her joy. She described being there as the best experience of her life. Remembering the event lifted her spirits every time she told the story.

40

Kintsukuroi

Kintsukuroi is a type of Japanese porcelain considered more valuable than a perfect, never-broken piece of porcelain because of the gold or silver used to mend it. Our own lives are much like kintsukuroi. By the time we reach adulthood, everyone has experienced breaking and mending. None of us is "never broken."

Do we perceive the breaking and mending process as one that makes us more valuable or one that devalues us? Do we look at the pieces of our lives and see their artistic potential or just a pile of pieces? Veins of pain and the dark colors of our lives may add texture and beauty depending upon how we tell our stories. Sometimes we become part of the silver and gold that helps others mend their lives. Becoming kintsukuroi is something to celebrate.

Matt would have preferred to not have been an alcoholic for nine years. It caused pain to him and to those he loved. On the other hand, now that he has been sober for a decade, it is because of his mended brokenness that he is approachable. He volunteers at a rehabilitation center for addicts. There is nothing in another person's life that shocks him. Matt would not trade his gold scars for anything.

41

Sit in the Pit

It is sometimes necessary to climb down and sit in the pit with our friends who are struggling. When our friends are hurting, our caring presence is 85 percent of our value. We can all be present. The challenge is to leave our suggestions elsewhere for a while. This is the hard part: just listening.

We draw out our friend's story. We do not suggest how this may become a valuable experience or have a silver lining or is just like what happened to us once upon a time. We're simply present. If the story is on auto-repeat for months, our friend may need a counselor. Grief can become a toxic grievance.

Emma's son died of a rare illness. Friends brought meals, walked with her, picked up her daughter from school, and included her in social occasions. They hugged her when she cried and let her talk about her son when she wanted to. They did not judge her when she occasionally didn't show up for events. They called or visited instead. Emma eventually used her artistic gifts to paint uplifting mosaics on hospital walls, including a wall in the hospital where her son was treated. She credits her newfound sense of purpose to the quiet friends who sat in the pit with her while she grieved.

Marriage/
Partnering

42

Marriage Coaching

Marriage counseling often has a negative connotation: something is broken and needs fixing. Let's call it *marriage coaching* instead. Coaching is something everyone welcomes, often for skills we are already good at, such as playing a sport or leading a team at work. Just as we wouldn't give a car to a 16-year-old without driving instructions, we shouldn't set out in marriage confident that our intelligence and our love for each other will conquer all differences. We are not the exception.

Our wedding day is the first day of our most challenging relationship, one that we hope will last a lifetime. Most of us haven't seen it well modeled. Weddings are an industry. We spend a lot of money getting married, but there is little support for staying married, and many worthy but time-consuming factors, such as work and children, to pull us apart. If we're smart, we'll get coaching. After all, divorce is an industry, too.

Liz and Jordan, both with advanced degrees, were certain that they didn't need marriage coaching. For the first 10 years of their relationship, they focused on their careers and on their children, not on each other. Their "marriage tank" slowly emptied. When they finally met with a marriage counselor, they wished they had started coaching years before.

43

Below the Waterline

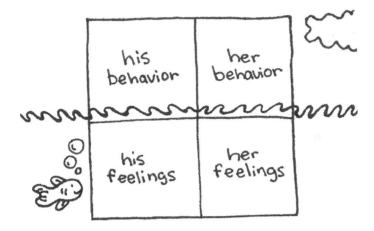

We can see fancy windows and decks on large cruise ships, but we know that the massive engine rooms below the waterline are what make the ships move. Similarly, the engine room of emotion is what makes people move, not our cognition. Couples often do not argue about the things they *think* they are arguing about. It's not about taking out the trash or picking up the kids or sex. It's about the emotions underneath the waterline—typically, feeling unappreciated, unsafe, or criticized.

Identifying our true emotion is a gift that we give to ourselves and our partners. We know that we have found this true emotion when our voices lower. We naturally reach toward our partner's quieter, more vulnerable feelings, instead of pulling away in anger. Revealing the true emotion for just a few minutes, or even a few seconds, is often long enough to resolve the tension between us.

"What's going on under the waterline?" became shorthand for Mark and Alia. It signaled their willingness to dive deeper, to explore the hurt or sad feelings "underneath" their argument. At first it was risky. Now it is a habit that shortens their disagreements and increases their intimacy.

44

The Rejection Coin

Criticism

Abandonment

We are hard-wired to dislike rejection. We experience rejection in one of two ways: abandonment or criticism, two sides of the same coin. This rejection coin is what virtually every argument is about. We typically partner with someone triggered by the opposite side of the coin. Which side of the rejection coin triggers you more? Ask your spouse (or teen) the same question.

We sometimes experience abandonment as being "not heard, unimportant, not seen, not cared about, or invisible" and criticism as being "judged, belittled, and never good enough." People look at each other differently when they understand that no one likes the rejection coin. This is not pathology. It is our basic human desire to avoid abandonment and criticism.

Nicole chased Caleb into his home office when he avoided their difficult conversations. Nicole thought that Caleb was uncaring and insensitive. Caleb perceived Nicole as aggressive and demanding. When they realized that Caleb hated criticism and Nicole feared abandonment, Nicole learned to say things more gently and Caleb learned to stay present in the room. Seeing each other's sensitivities as opposite sides of the same coin enabled them to understand each other better in moments of stress.

45

The Marriage Castle

We build our invisible marriage castle together on a patch of bare ground beginning on our wedding day. The building blocks are the traditions from our childhood, our behaviors, our routines, and the people we decide to welcome inside. It's important to talk about people and behaviors that we *don't* want in our castle, too.

Our relationships need to be defended and protected against invasion. The old images of marriage as a garden or a safe haven aren't strong enough. Demanding work schedules, the Internet, in-laws, and extended time apart are just a few of the challenges that are lobbed regularly into our castles. We need strong drawbridges to close the door for family time. We need to stock the moat with piranha to protect against unwelcome guests.

Everett and Priya both grew up in difficult families. They were afraid of committing to a long-term relationship. Designing their castle helped them intentionally build walls against yelling and excessive alcohol use that had hurt them as children. They included things that they wished they'd had as kids such as family dinners and community service projects.

46

Ignorance, Not Malevolence

Spouses are more often ignorant than malevolent. Your partner's intentions are more likely benign than harmful. The challenge is that our brains are wired to scan for danger. Our default response is to assume malevolence. He or she doesn't care/isn't there/is selfish/intends to hurt me. This is a hard rut to pave over in the brain once it has been well worn. Reminding ourselves that our partner probably doesn't intend harm or neglect is worth its weight in relationship gold. It calms our thought processes and helps us choose our words more thoughtfully.

Spouses are rarely as relationally intuitive as we wish they were. It helps to ask specifically for what we want. If we're getting nowhere, we can ask our partner how to make a request that will elicit a "yes" answer. A change in tone, word choice, and timing can make the difference. This applies to everything from affection to household tasks. We each have a preferred style and time of day that is optimal for receiving requests.

After years of hoping Rob would "get it," his wife, Alfa, learned to email him about specific tasks. Rob could put them on his calendar and feel like her hero instead of a villain. Susannah prefers that her partner, Mario, and her kids send her texts. She doesn't "do problems" after 10pm except for emergencies. Jon likes face-to-face requests from Crystal, preferably after his first cup of coffee. Learning their partners' preferred modes of communication and assuming ignorance rather than malevolence has made their households more harmonious.

47

Connection & Safety

During moments of marital stress, each of us favors either *connection* or *safety*. Both are essential to relationships. We typically choose a partner with the opposite priority because we are attracted to his or her complementary personality. Which is your priority? *Connectors* tend to be effervescent and outgoing. Partners who prioritize *safety* are usually reliable and steady.

The challenge arises during inevitable disagreements when the one who favors connection pursues an argument the way a dog pursues a bone and the one who favors safety withdraws behind a stone wall. One yells and the other won't talk. The more connectors won't let go, the more partners who prioritize safety retreat. This often escalates into an infinity loop of unhappiness.

Though it is difficult in the moment, when we remember that the "attacker" really wants *connection,* and the "stone wall" longs for safety, we can shorten our arguments and become allies.

Jordan and Caitlin were at each other's throats until they understood that Jordan was desperate for connection and Caitlin wanted safety. Prior to that, the more Jordan "came after" Caitlin, the more Caitlin "ran away." Seeing each other's need as 100 percent normal changed their perception of each other from hostile to compassionate.

48

From Land Mines to the I.C.U.

No one intentionally trips a land mine, but we frequently do so by accident in relationships. Partner A does or says something that trips a land mine and blows up Partner B. Outraged, Partner B lobs back a verbal grenade and blows up Partner A. Grenades fly back and forth. Both lie bleeding on the ground, expecting the other to provide care: an apology, a hand up, a glass of water. We continue to bleed as we argue about who started it.

A marital fight is like walking into a field of land mines. Imagine that we could be immediately transported to a hospital's I.C.U. as we would hope to be if we were hit by grenades. No one would be yelling. A medical team would be caring for us. We'd ask each other gently, "How are you doing?" We'd be grateful to be alive.

Jeff and Anita learned to go straight to the Intensive Care Unit with minimal damage when an argument started. They took turns saying, "I think I just tripped a land mine" or "Did I just trip a land mine?" Their teens adopted the same language to work things out with their parents and with each other.

49

Marriage 1.0, 2.0, 3.0

During the course of our relationship, we may be in our second, third or even sixth marriage to our first spouse. Investing in the person that our spouse is becoming is the most important investment in our economic portfolio. Relationships are no more static than financial investments, and they are much more important to our emotional well-being. We either intentionally support and move toward each other, or we drift apart.

The marriage of two grandparents is not the same marriage that they had as newlyweds. Relationships have seasons: dating, being newly married, having young kids, navigating a major move, coping with new jobs, sending kids to college, empty nesting, grieving the death of one's own parents, and dealing with the aging process. Each season is a chapter with its own number.

Relationships with no crises are highly unusual. Betrayals and the loss of a child are two of the hardest, but even the most difficult experiences do not have to be the death knell for a relationship. Relationships, like skin, are stronger where there is a scar. Being honest, embracing humility, and taking responsibility for personal growth are the tools to make marriage 2.0 or 3.0 stronger than marriage 1.0.

Julianne and Kyle's marriage had three near-death experiences: a serious financial mistake, the death of a child, and Julianne's addiction to pain killers after surgery. After 43 years of marriage, Julianne and Kyle are both grateful that someone normalized near-death experiences for them when they were a young couple.

50

Cell Phones Can't Charge Each Other

There is a romantic notion that a spouse can be "my every-thing." This idea is false. Our spouse cannot be our 24/7 charging station. Nor can we plug into ourselves. Couples need a wide circle of friends and advisors, as well as a tran-scendent source of strength, to provide meaning to life.

Contemplative practices and faith can remind us that we are part of a larger, loving community. These practices encourage us and challenge us to become our best selves.

Love cannot be solely self-generated or demanded from our partner when our own battery is low. It takes time and community to cultivate.

By developing a broad network of supportive relationships and a source of meaning beyond ourselves, we can override our human tendency to default to fear—including fear that our partner is somehow at fault for not meeting our every need.

Aaron and Whitney have a wide circle of trustworthy friends and share a meditation practice as part of their faith. They believe in a source of love bigger than themselves. When Aaron lost his job and Whitney developed a serious illness during the same year, they had a "charging station" large enough to power them up.

⑤⓵

L.O.V.E.

We have been trained to solve relationship problems the way we'd solve any other problem. This is what got us good grades in school and promotions at work. However, our ability to fix the problem is not what our partner wants when he or she is upset. Rather, he or she wants to be seen and heard.

An easy way to know what to do is remember the acronym **L.O.V.E.**

Listen twice as much as you want to listen. **Open** space for your partner to talk more by asking what else happened.

Validate that what upset your partner really happened and is worthy of concern. ("That was a rough morning!") And **Empathize** by sharing how you would have felt in that situation. ("I would have been angry, too.")

Initially, practicing **L.O.V.E.** may be counterintuitive. When we treat others with **L.O.V.E**, it calms their distress and often enables them to discover their own solutions.

Ian and Amanda are both doctors. Professionally, they have impressive toolkits. It wasn't easy for them to learn to keep their toolkits closed—until they began practicing L.O.V.E. with each other. "I'm ready for your suggestions" is their way of signaling to each other that they feel sufficiently heard to engage in problem-solving.

52

Polka Dot Jackets

Imagine that a woman was assaulted by a man wearing a polka dot jacket when she was 24. She marries a few years later and asks her husband never to wear polka dots. Obviously, there is nothing wrong with polka dots, but her husband might feel judged by her request until he understands their association with her past hurt.

We all have our "polka dot jackets." They include anything in our lives that has caused us pain. Sharing our "polka dot jackets" with our partner builds intimacy. Honoring each other's "polka dot jackets" builds trust. It is not a matter of morality; it is simple kindness.

Sally was raised by an alcoholic father. Her husband Nathan's drinking was not out of control, but Sally commented on it often. Nathan was annoyed by Sally's nagging. When he learned that this was a "polka dot jacket" for her, not a matter of right and wrong, he no longer felt judged. Out of love for Sally, he willingly limited his alcohol consumption to the amount that made her comfortable.

Greg's mother yelled at him when he was young. When his partner, Shauna, raised her voice, Greg would back away. Shauna became angry because she thought her voice was within normal range. Understanding Greg's "polka dot jacket" made it easier for her to speak more softly. She no longer felt criticized.

Costumes

In moments of marital stress, humor defuses tension. When your partner acts defensively or displays what you consider to be a "character defect," it can be helpful to reframe what you see: consider that your spouse has put on a costume in self-defense. Look for the fearful person underneath your spouse's costume.

Each of us puts on a costume when we feel threatened, typically an aggressive one or a protective one. What costume do you put on? Do you become a ferocious grizzly bear, a jaguar, a dictator, or King Kong? Or do you put on a suit of armor, a turtle shell, a rock, or an ostrich costume?

Costumes are removable, not part of our character. Knowing this can change stressful moments into opportunities to help each other (and our children) with costume changes.

Louise shouted at her partner, "You're an iceberg. I can only get to 10 percent of you!" Connor parried, "And you're a giant sponge. I can never fill you up!" The visual was so powerful and funny that they both laughed. The iceberg and the sponge became their single-word ways of letting each other know when they felt abandoned or overwhelmed. This comical visual allowed them to give one another what was helpful.

⑤④

The 1-to-10 Scale

Every couple encounters inevitable conflicts regarding how to support each other in daily life. We all have an invisible 1-to-10 scale of how important an event or a behavior is to us. We also have a 1-to-10 cost scale of how difficult it would be to accommodate our partner's requests. Putting both numbers on the table and talking about them can be a quick way to resolve tension.

If going to the event is an 8 priority for Anna and a 4 inconvenience for Noah, it makes sense for Noah to join

Anna. If, on the other hand, it costs Noah a 10 to rearrange his schedule, Anna will probably see that it makes sense for him not to attend. Obviously, every request can't be a 10. A general rule of thumb is to do everything we can to accommodate our partner's 9's and 10's, weighing carefully the costs to ourselves.

During Dan's busy season at work, Adriana's family came from overseas to celebrate her birthday. Dan had an important client meeting that evening. He asked Adriana for her 1-10 scale number. She said 10. For Dan, the importance of his meeting was a 7. He didn't want to miss his meeting, but he knew that his associate could handle it. He went to her party. Dan and Adriana use the 1-10 scale frequently with each other and with their children to keep decisions from becoming disputes.

Parenting

55

The Red Zone

The Red Zone is the season in life when parents are holding down demanding jobs *and* raising young kids. It is also the season of "lockdown" when parents have little chance to travel. They move around with a U-Haul of kid paraphernalia in tow. Sleep is often a mirage. It is historically the least happy season of marriage. It's normal to feel enormous stress at this time.

We are culturally encouraged to elevate our children and our jobs above our marriages. Watch for this drift if you want your partner to be there when your 18-year house-guests (kids) grow up. Say *no* to as many additional responsibilities as possible. Delete, defer, and delegate. Each *yes* takes time directly from your marriage, children, and sleep. Once you have chosen your priorities, check in with your family periodically to see if their experience matches your intent.

Paul was a college athlete and a gregarious man. When his four children were young, he limited his athletic pursuits to basic fitness, and focused his social life on activities that included his wife and children. He did as little overnight business travel as possible to run his company. Paul's decisions during the Red Zone allow him today to share a wide array of meaningful activities with his wife of 30 years, including athletics, travel, and friends.

56

Parent Your Best Friend's Child

My Friend's Kids

Pausing to consider how we would respond if our child belonged to our best friend moves our egos out of the way so that we can be firm and calm. It takes our fear of being an inadequate parent out of the equation. We would not let our friend's child act rudely or get hurt. Take a deep breath and picture what you would say or do for someone else's child—and then do the same for your own child.

Every parent worries about discipline. Setting boundaries and consequences is hard—and harder still when we fear that we might fail at it. Imagining that our children belong to someone else makes it easier to set and maintain appropriate boundaries. It allows us to handle children's inevitable moments of misbehavior without taking it personally.

Will used this framework to send his only child to a treatment center for drug addiction. When he considered what he would do for his nephew, he saw that there was nothing else he could do at home to fix the problem for his son.

Shannon's daughter screamed for candy in the grocery store checkout line. People stared. Shannon pretended for a moment that her daughter was the child of her best friend, Julia. Julia's son, Philip, could be a handful, too. Shannon felt less alone. She imagined what she would say to Philip and said those words to her daughter. It worked.

57

Affirm, Affirm, Affirm

By the time our children turn 18, they have absorbed every-thing we have taught or modeled for them. They can pre-dict how we would respond to most questions or statements. They can mimic us mercilessly.

We have tried to praise their efforts rather than their outcomes. We have tried to make our boundaries few and firm, and our consequences fit the crime. We have tried to raise children who feel empowered, but not entitled. It has been exhausting and exhilarating. The good news is that after age 18, unless we see behavior that is immoral, illegal, or dangerous, our job is to affirm, affirm, affirm.

Parents worry about their children's choices of mates, jobs, and behaviors. Our kids will choose mates not on our short list, have jobs that didn't exist when we were their age, and behave in ways that surprise us. They have seen how we handle relationships, careers, and integrity issues. It is time to affirm their own abilities to make decisions, handle problems, and choose a good partner. Our fear does them no good. Our affirmation quiets our fearful brains and theirs—and helps them figure out their next steps.

When Tyler was a high school senior, his father thought he wasn't working up to his academic potential. They fought constantly and sought counseling. What Tyler needed was his dad's affirmation that he was a hard worker, capable of doing whatever he set his mind to. When Dad learned to highlight his son's successes, their relationship improved, and his son was motivated to pursue his own dreams.

58

Health & Safety

Many decisions that our children make are a matter of taste or preference. Studying on the floor or showering at midnight may be unusual, but neither is life-threatening. The same is true for wearing all-black clothing in high school. However, if the issue is a matter of health or safety, we parents make the decisions. They are not negotiable.

Of course, setting limits will annoy our children. Our toddlers and teens become angry when we enforce boundaries. We are *both* doing our jobs—theirs to push the limits, and ours to keep them alive. We both get A's.

This conflict starts at age 2 and ends at age 18, or when our kids no longer live under our roof. It's tiring and complicated. This simple mantra of *health and safety* helps us determine when to hold the line and when to acquiesce to generational differences of style.

Stacy prepared different food and studied different subjects than her parents would have chosen for her. Her parents adjusted because neither decision was a matter of health and safety.

Jesse's friend, Cody, stopped by to give Jesse a ride to a party. Jesse's mom could tell that Cody had been drinking alcohol. She refused to let Jesse drive with him on health and safety grounds. Jesse was annoyed. She was firm. It was simple.

59

Build a Team

It is wise to encourage children to cultivate a team of people beyond their parents to whom they can turn for advice. It's ideal to begin this when they are in grade school. At first, their team may include relatives, older friends, teachers, and grandparents. As they age, it will include peers and people whom we don't know. The concept of building a team allows them to consider who is wise and trustworthy. This pays dividends in adolescence when parents are not usually popular.

It helps our children when we, too, have a team. Our team might consist of people we call when we have difficult decisions to make, or when crises arise. Our adult team keeps us from relying too heavily on ourselves, our spouses, or our children for support. Letting our children see that we have a team of advisors and encouraging them to have their own teaches them the strength of community.

When Kristin was applying to colleges, her parents suggested that she ask three people on her team to read and comment on her college essays. When Samuel had questions about his sexuality, his coach and his aunt were helpful resources. When Sean was considering a career move, his mom's friend was his go-to person. These young adults made more confident decisions because their teams were bigger than just their parents.

60

If You Need an Answer Now, It's No

Children, and especially teens, can badger parents with requests. "Can I have ice cream? Can you take me to Arielle's house? Can I have 20 dollars?" Such requests can be overwhelming, especially if we have more than one child.

Assuming that a request is reasonable, a simple way to keep our sanity is to reply, "If you have to have an answer now, it's 'no,' but if you can wait an hour (or until tomorrow) it might be 'yes.'" This response keeps us calm and teaches our children to delay gratification. They may also figure out another solution during the wait.

Often, we worry that not meeting our children's needs will scar them for life. In fact, we are often helping them by giving them space to be resourceful. Especially in the area of self-entertainment, downtime is vital to creativity and imagination.

"Kevin, if you can wait until I finish this phone call, I will be happy to help you with your Legos. If you keep bothering me now, I won't."

"Dustin, the only answer I can give you now is no because I need some time to think about it. Your mother and I will talk it over and let you know tomorrow."

61

Rescues

Rescues for forgotten homework, athletic equipment, lunch money, or other things that kids forget work well when we clarify the number of rescues that we will be responsible for ahead of time. This teaches our children to plan ahead and manage their own stuff. Rescues should diminish in frequency as our children mature. For example, once a week in grade school, once a month in middle school, and once a quarter in high school. When we are notified that something has been forgotten, we can ask our child if this is the way she wants to use her rescue this week/month/quarter.

Some rescues shouldn't happen. If we get in the way of a natural or legal consequence of our children's actions, we may deny them the gift of learning how to make better choices in the future.

George coached his son's football team. Pete often forgot part of his gear. George limited the times he dashed home to get some essential piece of Pete's equipment. The hard lesson came when the team traveled to an away-game. Pete sat on the sidelines for the whole game because he had forgotten his helmet. He had used up his rescues. He never forgot his equipment again.

Sandra heard her parents tell the police that she wasn't home. She was actually hiding in her bedroom after crashing her car into a fence. Her parents didn't want Sandra to have a DUI for underage drinking. She has since been in and out of three rehabs.

62

A Tulip or an Oak Tree?

Parents wonder when to help and when to let children, especially teens, work things out for themselves. Too often we jump in when our children would do well to work it out on their own. We want so much to clear the roadway for our children; however, like us, they learn from adversity and challenges.

If we see our child struggling with a problem or a decision, we can ask her if she feels like a tulip about to be blown over by the strong wind, or if she feels like an oak tree with roots deep enough to figure it out on her own. Her answer might not come right away, but by asking her the question, she can take responsibility for the amount of adult support she wants.

Feel free to invent other metaphors for vulnerability and strength. A bug about to be squished versus an eagle sheltering in the cleft of a tree during a storm might appeal more to your child.

Jorge was a junior in high school crying quietly alone in his room after being cut from the basketball team. His dad sat down next to him and asked him if he felt like a drowning puppy or a wet dog. Jorge told him he felt like a puppy. It was time for some fatherly advice.

63

Luxuries & Emergencies

Generally speaking, fiscal independence is a goal for young adults. This is especially important because other traditional markers of adulthood, such as marriage and child bearing, now often occur later in life. Supporting oneself financially is a major factor in developing a sense of autonomy.

Clearly, in seasons of transition, some financial support may be helpful—such as right after graduation from high school or college. It is important however that our support be limited and temporary so that we don't interfere with our adult children's sense of providing for themselves.

Paying for occasional luxuries or emergencies—such as a family vacation or a medical bill—doesn't undermine our adult children's efforts to fund their own lifestyles. These gifts are unexpected expressions of our love and care, not counted on to fund their daily cost of living. (How we define luxuries and emergencies is up to us.)

Stephen moved across the country after his wedding. A month before Christmas, he told his parents, "We won't be coming home for Christmas. It's not in our budget." His dad replied, "Having you here for Christmas might be a luxury for you, but it's an emergency for your mom and me." For the next few years, two plane tickets home were the couple's Christmas presents.

64

Changing the Legacy

Most parents worry that they're not doing enough for their children, particularly if they themselves grew up in a chaotic family. Many of us grew up with a model that we don't want to repeat. Our legacy is far more than the cash or things we leave behind for our children in our will. Our most important legacy is the childhood that our children remember. It shapes their adult lives more than any amount of money in their inheritance.

No one can move the legacy dial to perfect, but we can make it better, whatever that means to us. Parents who judge themselves harshly are often already improving on the way they grew up. We can ask ourselves: "Is the D I got from my parents now a B in my own kids' lives? Have I made changes in my own parenting to make a B- an A-? Am I willing to get coaching when I need it?" Emotional care is equally—if not more—important than physical care or economic circumstances.

Shannon worried about her parenting. Her therapist asked her how she thought her children would answer the question "does your mommy love you?" Shannon knew there was less shouting and more hugs in her family than there had been when she grew up. Shannon whispered, "Yes." Her advisor told her that was enough. If you are engaged in being a better parent, that is enough.

About the Author and Illustrator

Jill Woolworth and Wajih Chaudhry met in January 2017 when they were both students taking a class together at Stanford University. Jill admired Wajih's drawings. Wajih was interested in Jill's experience as a marriage and family therapist. Wajih agreed to illustrate the book that Jill had been compiling for several years. It was a seamless collaboration. *The Waterwheel* is the result.

During their collaboration, Wajih was a sophomore from Tennessee who hoped to build his career around creative design and neuroscience. Jill was a Partner in Stanford's Distinguished Career Institute, on sabbatical from her work at the Greenwich Center for Hope & Renewal in Greenwich, Connecticut.